JOHN CENA

BY ADAM STONE

BELLWETHER MEDIA · MINNEAPOLIS, MN

Are you ready to take it to the extreme?
Torque books thrust you into the action-packed world
of sports, vehicles, mystery, and adventure. These books
may include dirt, smoke, fire, and dangerous stunts.
WARNING : read at your own risk.

Library of Congress Cataloging-in-Publication Data

Stone, Adam.
  John Cena / by Adam Stone.
      p. cm. -- (Torque: pro wrestling champions)
  Includes bibliographical references and index.
  Summary: "Engaging images accompany information about John Cena. The combination of high-
interest subject matter and light text is intended for students in grades 3 through 7"--Provided by
publisher.
  ISBN 978-1-60014-636-7 (hardcover : alk. paper)
  1. Cena, John--Juvenile literature. 2. Wrestlers--United States--Biography--Juvenile literature. 3. Motion
picture actors and actresses--United States--Biography--Juvenile literature. I. Title.
  GV1196.C46S86 2011
  796.812092--dc22
  [B]   2011007903

This edition first published in 2012 by Bellwether Media, Inc.

Printed in the United States of America, North Mankato, MN.

080111   1187

CONTENTS

CHAMPIONSHIP MATCH

More than 70,000 wrestling fans stood and cheered at WrestleMania 26. John Cena entered the ring to wrestle for the World Wrestling Entertainment (WWE) Championship. He had to beat the current champion, Batista, to win the belt.

Batista took control of the match early. He hammered Cena with punches, slams, and other moves. Just when it looked like Cena was finished, he came charging back. He broke out of one of Batista's **submission holds** and got to his feet.

VITAL STATS

Wrestling Name: _ _ _ _ _ _ _ _ _ _ _ _ _John Cena

Real Name: _ _ _ _ _ _ _ _John Felix Anthony Cena

Height: _ _ _ _ _ _ _ _ _6 feet, 1 inch (1.9 meters)

Weight: _ _ _ _ _ _ _ _240 pounds (110 kilograms)

Started Wrestling: _ _ _ _ _ _ _ _ _ _ _ _ _ _2000

Finishing Move: _ _ _ _ _ _ Attitude Adjustment

The crowd cheered for Cena as the wrestlers battled. Cena slammed Batista to the mat with an **Attitude Adjustment**, but Batista escaped the pin. Then Cena used a submission hold on Batista. He bent Batista's leg at a painful angle. Batista soon **tapped out**. Cena was the new WWE Champion!

WRESTLEMA

BATISTA

7

WHO IS JOHN CENA?

John Felix Anthony Cena was born on April 23, 1977 in West Newbury, Massachusetts. He was a star athlete growing up. Cena liked to watch Hulk Hogan, Ultimate Warrior, Shawn Michaels, and other wrestling stars on television. However, he never planned to become a wrestler. He wanted to play football.

Cena began lifting weights when he was 15. After high school, he went to college in Springfield, Massachusetts. He was an offensive lineman on the football team. Teammates voted Cena team captain because of his skill and leadership. Cena graduated with a degree in **exercise physiology**.

QUICK HIT!

Cena was a limousine driver for a while after college.

In 2000, Cena moved to California to be a **bodybuilder**. He met someone at the gym who was training to be a wrestler. Cena decided to start training. He went to a wrestling school called Ultimate University. Later, he joined a league called Ultimate Pro Wrestling (UPW). He wrestled as The Prototype. Cena was very popular with the fans.

BECOMING
A CHAMPION

QUICK HIT!

Cena has starred in
a few movies, including
12 Rounds and *The Marine*.

In 2001, WWE signed Cena to a **developmental contract.** He wrestled in a small league called Ohio Valley Wrestling (OVW). Cena first wrestled for WWE in 2002. He fought Kurt Angle, the WWE Champion at the time. It was a close match, but Cena lost. The match made Cena a fan favorite. He had become a **face**.

Cena has been both a face and a **heel** in WWE. He has had **feuds** with Chris Jericho, Triple H, and other wrestling stars. He has won both the WWE United States Championship and the WWE Championship. In 2008, he outlasted 29 other wrestlers to win the **Royal Rumble**.

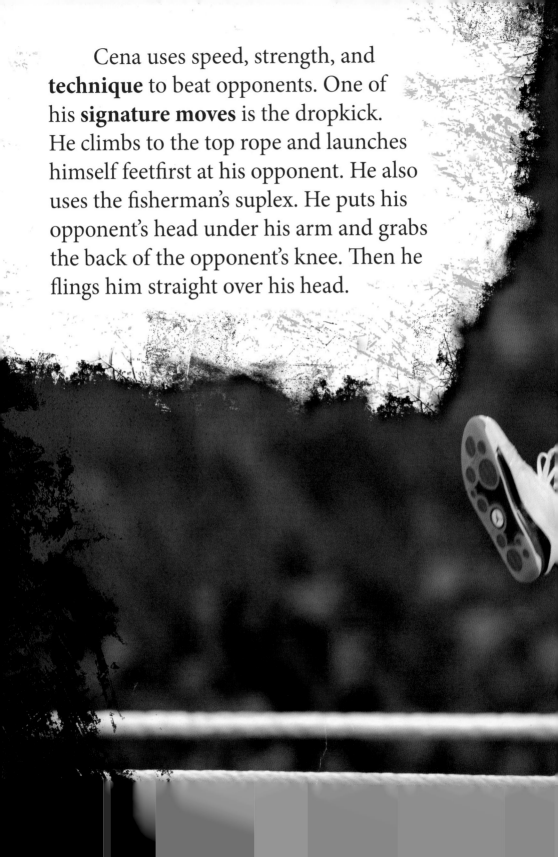

Cena uses speed, strength, and **technique** to beat opponents. One of his **signature moves** is the dropkick. He climbs to the top rope and launches himself feetfirst at his opponent. He also uses the fisherman's suplex. He puts his opponent's head under his arm and grabs the back of the opponent's knee. Then he flings him straight over his head.

GLOSSARY

Attitude Adjustment—Cena's finishing move; Cena lifts his opponent over his shoulders and slams him down to the mat.

bodybuilder—someone who lifts weights to build up a lot of muscle

developmental contract—an agreement in which a wrestler signs with WWE but first wrestles in a smaller league to gain experience and develop skills

exercise physiology—the study of exercise and the human body

face—a wrestler seen by fans as a hero

feuds—long-lasting conflicts between two people or teams

finishing move—a wrestling move meant to finish off an opponent so that he can be pinned

heel—a wrestler seen by fans as a villain

Royal Rumble—a popular WWE battle between 30 wrestlers; instead of starting all at once, wrestlers join the battle every few minutes.

signature moves—moves that a wrestler is famous for performing

submission holds—wrestling moves that put an opponent in great pain or risk of injury; submission holds usually cause the opponent to tap out.

tapped out—quit a match due to pain or injury caused by a submission hold

technique—skillful and proper performance of moves

TO LEARN MORE

AT THE LIBRARY

Black, Jake. *The Ultimate Guide to WWE.* New York, N.Y.: Grosset & Dunlap, 2010.

O'Shei, Tim. *John Cena.* Mankato, Minn.: Capstone Press, 2010.

Shields, Brian. *John Cena.* New York, N.Y.: DK, 2009.

ON THE WEB

Learning more about John Cena is as easy as 1, 2, 3.

1. Go to www.factsurfer.com.

2. Enter "John Cena" into the search box.

3. Click the "Surf" button and you will see a list of related Web sites.

With factsurfer.com, finding more information is just a click away.

INDEX

The images in this book are reproduced through the courtesy of: Film Magic / Getty Images, front cover, p. 16; Associated Press, pp. 4-5; John Smolek, p. 7; David Seto, pp. 8-9; Brian Rasic / Rex USA, pp. 10-11; Wire Image / Getty Images, pp. 12-13; c. 20thC. Fox / Everett / Rex USA, pp. 14-15; Juan Martinez, p. 17; Getty Images, pp. 18-19, 20, 21.